Yellow
Book
3

JUNIOR
READING Start

Iambooks

© 2011 I am Books

Published by
I am Books
327-32   1116ho, Daeroung Techno Town 12cha
Gasan-dong, Kumcheon-gu, Seoul, Korea 153-802
TEL 82-2-6343-0999
FAX 82-2-6343-0995~6
www.iambooks.co.kr

Publisher	Sangwook Oh, Sunghyun Shin
Author	TIMES CORE The Junior Times
Editor	Sungwon Lee, Dahhyun Gang, Jinhee Lee
Design	Mijung Oh, Ran Park
Illustrations	Soyoung Cho
Marketing	Shindong Jang, Shinkuk Jo, Jinhee Jung, Misun Jang

ISBN 978-89-6398-057-7 64740

Yellow
Book
3

JUNIOR
READING Start

How to **Study** This Book

01 Before reading articles, listen to audio files carefully two or three times.

02 Underline words that you are not familiar with, reading aloud the article.

03 Read the article one more time, making a guess the meaning of words.

04 Look up the dictionary to find out the meaning of words.

05 Memorize words that you don't know and try to solve the word tip quiz.

06 Read the article once again and answer the questions.

07 Lastly, listen to the audio file one more time focusing on the words you've learned.

CONTENTS

World's Oldest Twins

Guinness World Records said that Ena Pugh and Lily Millward are the oldest twins in the world. The twin sisters were born on January 4, 1910 in the UK. They became 101 years old in 2011! They are still very healthy. They enjoy shopping together every week. They say that the secret to living a long life is laughter. If you want to live a long life, laugh a lot like the world's oldest twin sisters!

Staff reporter Daniel Chang

Use the words below and complete the sentences.

the oldest / sisters / twins / 101 years
healthy / laughter / enjoy / born

(a) Who are they?

→ They are _____ in the world.

(b) How old are they in 2011?

→ They are _____ old.

(c) According to them, what is the secret for living a long life?

→ They say it is _____.

Word Tip

▌ the oldest	▌ twins	▌ be born	▌ enjoy ~ing
_____	_____	_____	_____
▌ secret	▌ 장수하다, 오래 살다	▌ 웃음	▌ 웃다
_____	_____	_____	_____
▌ ~처럼			
_____			

 **02** Question **Grammar**

Circle the right answer to make the sentence correct.

(a) The twin sisters were born [**on** / **at** / **from**] January 4, 1910 in the UK.

(b) They are still very [**healthy** / **health** / **healthily**].

(c) They enjoy [**to shop** / **shopping** / **shops**] together every week.

(d) If you want to live a long life, laugh a lot [**like** / **despite** / **except**] the world's oldest twin sisters.

 **03** Question **Writing Ⅱ**

Write your own story describing the picture below.

Hint: Be creative!

Who are they?

_____

_____

_____

_____

_____

_____

_____

_____

 Question **Vocabulary**

Let's finish the cross word puzzle below related to the story.

Across
① Strong and not suffering from any diseases
② Two people who look alike

Down
③ Something that you don't want to tell everybody
④ Consists of 12 months

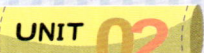

I am Working Hard for the President!

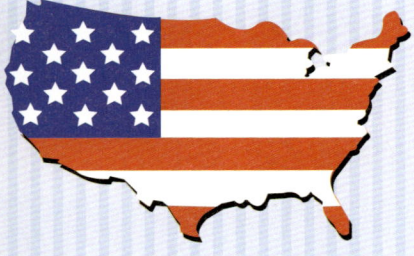

Hines Ward is working for the U.S. President Barack Obama. Mr. Ward is a Korean-American football player. He was born to a Korean mother and an African-American father in 1976. On September 16, 2010, Mr. Obama chose him as one of his advisors. Mr. Ward is still giving the President advice on many things.

Staff reporter Erica Choi

Comprehension I

Read each question and find the right answer.

(a) What is the main topic of the article?

① Hines Ward was chosen as the adviser of the U.S. President.

② Hines Ward was chosen as the superstar in America.

③ Hines Ward gives the courage to Korean people.

④ The U.S. President gives the courage to Hines Ward.

(b) Write down three words that begin with "F" in the article.

① _____

② _____

③ _____

(c) What is Heins Ward doing for the President?

Mr. Ward is giving the President __ __ __ __ __ __ on many things.

Word Tip			
▮ work for	▮ Korean–American	▮ football player	▮ be born
_____	_____	_____	_____
▮ 아프리카계 미국인	▮ A를 B로 선택하다	▮ 고문, 조언자	▮ 조언, 충고
_____	_____	_____	_____

 **Question** ## Vocabulary

Choose the right word to complete each sentence.

(a) Hines Ward is working for the U.S. _____ Barack Obama.

   ① Football player

   ② Scientist

   ③ President

   ④ Singer

(b) He was _____ _____ a Korean mother and an African-American father in 1976.

   ① born by

   ② born into

   ③ born in

   ④ born to

(c) Mr. Ward is still giving the President _____ on many things.

   ① advisor

   ② courage

   ③ answers

   ④ advice

 **Question** **Comprehension II**

Look at the picture below and then answer the questions.

(a) What is he doing?

① He is talking into the microphone.

② He is talking on the phone.

③ He is crying sadly.

④ He is closing his eyes.

(b) What does he do?

① He is a famous professor in America.

② He is a famous artist in America.

③ He is a famous football player in America.

④ He is a famous chef in America.

(c) Choose the word that explains "The things you tell others to be helpful for them."

① adventure   ② discourage

③ advice   ④ waste

Do People in North Korea Enjoy Eating Hamburgers, too?

Most children around the world love eating hamburgers. They are very delicious! But do people in North Korea also enjoy eating hamburgers? Yes, they do! The first fast food restaurant was opened in Pyongyang in June 2010. The restaurant sells hamburgers, fish burgers, and waffles. These foods are gaining huge popularity among North Koreans. The restaurant will soon sell hot dogs, too!

Staff reporter Daniel Chang

Let's look at the picture and fill in the blanks.

Hint: Answers are in the article.

(a) Most children _____ the world love eating hamburgers.

(b) But do people in North Korea also _____ eating hamburgers?

(c) The first fast food restaurant was _____ in Pyongyang in 2010.

(d) These foods are gaining huge _____ among North Koreans.

(e) The restaurant will _____ sell hot dogs, too!

Word Tip			
▌delicious	▌fast food	▌restaurant	▌sell
_____	_____	_____	_____
▌와플	▌큰 인기를 얻다	▌~사이에서	▌곧, 머지않아
_____	_____	_____	_____

 **Question** # Vocabulary II

Connect each picture to the correct meaning.

delicious

ⓐ

① To find pleasure in doing or experiencing something

enjoy

ⓑ

② With a very pleasant taste or smell

popularity

ⓒ

③ To become famous or well-liked

 **Writing**

Look at the picture below and write your own answers.

Hint: Be creative!

(a) Where are the people eating their food?

→ They are eating _____.

(b) What does the restaurant sell?

→ The restaurant sells _____.

(c) Are fast food restaurants popular among North Koreans?

→ They are _____ among North Koreans.

Let's Go Travel!

Do you like traveling? Many people like to travel with their family or friends. There are many nice places to go. Going somewhere new is a lot of fun!

Traveling is a wonderful way to relax. It is also a great chance to have fun with your family. You can also learn new things. You can meet new people, too. Of course eating something new is also a lot of fun! Plan a fun trip with your family. You can travel by car, train or even airplane! So, where do you want to go this fall?

Staff reporter Dan Chun

Conversation

Complete the sentences by filling in the blanks.

(a) Hi, my name is Clair. Do you like to _____? Today, I would like to tell you how _____ traveling is!

(b) Traveling is a wonderful way to _____. It is also a great _____ to have fun with your family.

(c) Going _____ new and of course eating _____ new are also a lot of fun.

(d) You can also _____ new things and _____ new people by traveling.

(e) You can travel by car, train or _____ airplane! Why don't you plan a fun trip with your _____ this fall?

Word Tip

▌travel	▌place	▌somewhere	▌fun
_____	_____	_____	_____
▌wonderful	▌relax	▌chance	▌재미있게 놀다, 즐기다
_____	_____	_____	_____
▌물론	▌새로운 무엇(어떤 것)	▌계획하다	▌기차
_____	_____	_____	_____
▌비행기			
_____			

 **Vocabulary** I

Let's learn how to spell the important words in the article!

(a) **T** __ __ __ __ __

(b) **R** __ __ __

(c) **C** __ __ __ __ __

(d) **P** __ __ __

 **Question** # Vocabulary II

Find the words below that are related to vacation.

Tent / Noisy / Airplane / Busy / Barbeque
Relax / Pencil / Angry / Camera / Wallet

(a) **T** __ __ __

(b) **A** __ __ __ __ __ __ __

(c) **B** __ __ __ __ __ __ __

(d) **R** __ __ __ __

(e) **C** __ __ __ __ __

Your Birthday Is a Special Day!

When is your birthday? You celebrate this day once a year. Your birthday is a very special day! It is the day you were born. Let's celebrate your day!

What do you do on your birthday? Many children all over the world celebrate their special day with their family and friends: You invite your friends to your house. Then, you eat delicious food and cake with your family and friends. You also receive cards and gifts from them! Yes, it is the best day of the year. Why don't you make special plans for your birthday?

Staff reporter Dan Chun

Read the questions and answer the following.

(a) Look at the words below.

Cake   House   Gift   Year   Card

Which words can be used to talk about your birthday? Choose three words.

_____, _____, _____

(b) Find the three words that start with "F" in the article.

① _____

② _____

③ _____

(c) Which word has the opposite meaning of "Receive?"

G __ __ __

Word Tip

▌birthday	▌celebrate	▌all over the world	▌invite
_____	_____	_____	_____
▌맛있는	▌받다	▌~하는 것이 어때?	▌계획
_____	_____	_____	_____

02 Question **Writing**

Let's make sentences by filling in the blanks, using the words below.

> celebrate / special / invite / friends / delicious

(a) You **c** __ __ __ __ __ __ __ __ your birthday once a year.

(b) You eat **d**__ __ __ __ __ __ __ food with your **f**__ __ __ __ __ __.

(c) Why don't you **i**__ __ __ __ __ many people for your **s**__ __ __ __ __ __ day?

03 Question **Comprehension**

Look at the pictures. Mark "O" for the picture that looks happy and special. Mark "X" for the picture that looks unhappy.

a. (   )

b. (   )

c. (   )

d. (   )

04 Question **Structure**

Match up the pictures and words to make the right sentences.

You eat delicious food   ① with their family and friends.

Your birthday is   ② from your friends.

Many children celebrate
their special day   ③ on your birthday.

You receive cards and gifts   ④ a very special day.

Spending Time with Your Pet Makes You Happy

Do you have a pet at home? Doctors say that keeping pets is actually good for your health. This is because they can make you feel happier!

According to British doctors, spending time with your pet is a good way to beat stress. Many dog owners say that they feel better after spending time with their dogs. The doctors found in their study that playing with pets helped people calm down. "When you are stressed, spend time with your pet. Soon, you will feel much better!" said the doctors. When you feel down, why don't you go for a walk with your dog? Then you will feel much happier!

Staff reporter Liz Ahn

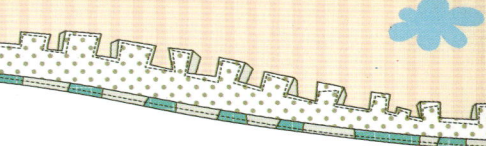

Read the questions and answer the following.

(a) Look at the words below.

Doctor   Pet   Owner

What item is talked about in the article?

_____

(b) Think of the words that start with the letter 'P'!

① _____

② _____

③ _____

(c) Why is spending time with a pet good?

_____.

Word Tip

▌pet	▌actually	▌health	▌according to
_____	_____	_____	_____
▌spend	▌way	▌owner	▌기분이 나아지다
_____	_____	_____	_____
▌발견하다, 알아내다	▌연구	▌진정하다, 마음이 가라앉다	▌스트레스를 받다
_____	_____	_____	_____
▌곧, 머지않아	▌마음이 울적하다		
_____	_____		

02 Question **Writing**

The following words were in the article. They are scrambled. Let's make sentences by filling in the blanks.

> beat / spending / down / walk / health

(a) Doctors say that keeping pets is actually good for your **h** __ __ __ __ __.

(b) According to British doctors, **s** __ __ __ __ __ __ __ time with your pet is a good way to **b** __ __ __ stress.

(c) When you feel **d** __ __ __, why don't you go for a **w** __ __ __ with your dog?

03 Question **Comprehension**

Look at the pictures. Mark 'O' for the picture that looks happy and healthy. Mark 'X' for the picture that looks unhappy and unhealthy.

a. (   )

b. (   )

c. (   )

d. (   )

Match up the pictures and phrases to make the right sentences.

Doctors say that   ⓐ

① why don't you go for a walk with your dog?

Spending time with your pet is ⓑ

② keeping pets is actually good for your health.

When you feel down,   ⓒ

③ a good way to beat stress.

Let's Ride a Bike!

Fall is a good season for a bike ride. Bike riding is a lot of fun! It is also good for your health. But wait! You need to know how to ride your bike safely.

First, wear your bike helmet. You need to protect your head. Next, wear bright clothes. It helps other people and cars on the road to see you easily. Always ride your bike in safe places. Don't go to the street where there are many cars. It is best to use bike-only lanes. When crossing a busy road, walk your bike across the street. Enjoy riding your bike safely this fall!

Staff reporter Daniel Chang

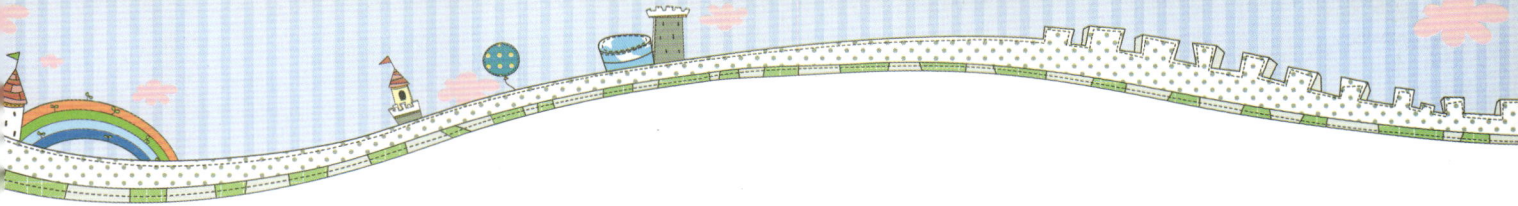

Writing

Fill in the blanks with the right words.

remember / protect / only / health
bright / walk

(a) You should wear a helmet to _____ your head.

(b) Bike riding is good for your _____.

(c) It is good to wear _____ clothes.

Word Tip

fall	season	bike	ride
_____	_____	_____	_____
be good for	health	wait	need to
_____	_____	_____	_____
안전하게	입다	헬멧	보호하다
_____	_____	_____	_____
밝은	옷	도로	쉽게
_____	_____	_____	_____

Comprehension

Look at the sentences below and decide whether they are true (o) or false (x).

(a) Winter is a good season for a bike ride.　　　　　　　O / X

(b) Wearing dark clothes helps other people and cars to see you easily.　　　　　　　O / X

(c) When crossing a busy road, walk your bike across the street.　　　　　　　O / X

Vocabulary I

Choose the right word to complete each sentence.

(a) Wear a helmet to protect your [**feet** / **head** / **shoulder**] .

(b) Bike riding is good for your [**health** / **brain** / **love**] .

(c) Always ride your bike in [**quiet** / **safe** / **dangerous**] places.

 **Question** **Vocabulary Ⅱ**

Let's find the words from the story in this word puzzle!

A	B	R	T	E	S	G	E	R	S
P	D	G	H	I	G	H	F	J	D
O	B	T	S	E	A	S	O	N	N
W	Q	H	J	K	M	A	O	U	V
T	E	R	T	G	H	F	I	U	B
U	P	P	R	O	T	E	C	T	O
L	O	U	I	F	H	N	D	H	H
A	V	D	F	E	G	J	K	L	U
N	C	V	B	R	I	G	H	T	L
E	B	N	M	H	D	S	A	W	E

Words

SAFE / SEASON / LANE

BRIGHT / PROTECT

It's Time to Read Books!

It's already October. It is still hot during the day. But it is cool in the morning and at night. Yes, fall is here! Fall is a beautiful season. It is also the perfect season to read books!

Do you like reading books? Reading books is very important for children. You can learn many things from books. You can learn about world history, famous people, and other countries' cultures. Fall is a wonderful season to read books. There are many good books you can choose from. Why don't you read lots of books this fall?

Staff reporter Liz Ahn

Read the questions and answer the following.

(a) Look at the words below.

> Books   History   People

Which item is talked about in the article?

_____

(b) Think of the words that start with the letter 'B'!

① _____

② _____

③ _____

④ _____

(c) Why is reading books important for children?

_____ .

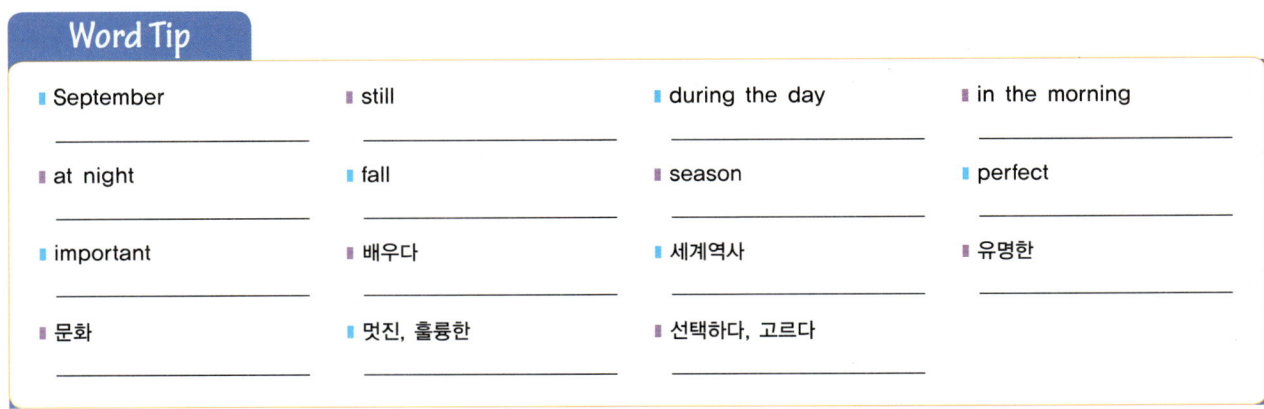

Word Tip			
▌September	▌still	▌during the day	▌in the morning
_____	_____	_____	_____
▌at night	▌fall	▌season	▌perfect
_____	_____	_____	_____
▌important	▌배우다	▌세계역사	▌유명한
_____	_____	_____	_____
▌문화	▌멋진, 훌륭한	▌선택하다, 고르다	
_____	_____	_____	

 **Question** **Writing**

The following words were in the article. They are scrambled. Let's make sentences by filling in the blanks.

history / perfect / choose / cultures

(a) It is also the **p** __ __ __ __ __ __ season to read books!

(b) You can learn about world **h** __ __ __ __ __ __, famous people, and other countries' **c** __ __ __ __ __ __ __ .

(c) There are many good books you can **c** __ __ __ __ __ from.

03 **Question** **Comprehension**

Look at the pictures. Mark 'O' for the picture that looks happy and healthy. Mark 'X' for the picture that looks unhappy and unhealthy.

a. ( )

b. ( )

 **Question** ## Structure

Match up the pictures and words to make the right sentences.

Fall is   ⓐ   ① a wonderful season to read books.

Reading books   ⓑ   ② many good books you can choose from.

There are   ⓒ   ③ is very important for children.

Learn from Your Mistakes!

Oops! Are you in trouble? Did you make a mistake? Don't worry. It's ok to make a mistake. In fact, you can learn many things from your mistakes!

No one is perfect. Everyone sometimes makes mistakes. Even your mom and dad make mistakes! It's true that it doesn't feel very good to make a mistake. But you know what? It is a good way to learn something! First, admit your mistake. Second, think about how it happened. Third, learn from your mistake and be careful not to make the same mistake again. Sometimes people even find new ways to solve problems by making mistakes!

Staff reporter Dan Chun

Read the questions and answer the following.

(a) Look at the words below.

> Disappoint   Admit   Scowl   Careful   Learn

Which words can be used to talk about learning from your mistakes?
Choose three words.

_____, _____, _____

(b) Find the three words that start with "M" in the article.

① _____

② _____

③ _____

(c) Which word has the opposite meaning of "Same"?

D __ __ __ __ __ __ __

Word Tip			
▌be in trouble	▌make a mistake	▌in fact	▌perfect
_____	_____	_____	_____
▌인정하다	▌조심하다	▌방법	▌문제를 풀다(해결하다)
_____	_____	_____	_____

 **Question 02** ## Writing

Let's make sentences by filling in the blanks, using the words below.

same / learn / fact / admit / mistake

(a) In __ __ __ __, you can __ __ __ __ __ many things from your mistakes!

(b) Learn from your __ __ __ __ __ __ __ and be careful not to make the __ __ __ __ mistake again.

(c) You must first __ __ __ __ __ your mistake.

Question 03 ## Comprehension

Look at the pictures. Mark "O" for the pictures that look happy. Mark "X" for the pictures that look worried.

a. (   )   b. (   )

c. (   )   d. (   )

 **Structure**

Match up the pictures and words to make the right sentences.

Your mom and dad   ⓐ

① make mistakes as well.

It's true that you don't feel very good   ⓑ

② to solve problems by making mistakes.

Learn from your mistake   ⓒ

③ and be careful not to make the same mistake again.

People can even find new ways   ⓓ

④ after making a mistake.

What Is the Sun?

Look at the sky. What can you see? Yes, you can see the sun! We can see it every day. But how much do you know about it? Let's learn some interesting facts about the sun!

The sun is a star. In fact, it is the most important star. Without the sun, there would be no life on Earth! The sun gives us light and heat. It is the closest star to the Earth. The sun is the center of our Solar System. All the planets orbit around it. The Earth rotates around the sun every 365 days. The sun is about 100 times bigger than the Earth. It weighs about 330,000 times more than the Earth. The sun is made up mostly of hydrogen.

Staff reporter Erica Choi

Complete the sentences by filling in the blanks.

(a) How **m** __ __ __ do you know about the sun?

(b) The sun is the **m** __ __ __ important star.

(c) The sun gives us light and **h** __ __ __.

(d) The sun is the **c** __ __ __ __ __ of our Solar System.

(e) The sun is **m** __ __ __ up mostly of hydrogen.

Word Tip			
▎look at	▎every day	▎interesting	▎in fact
▎without	▎life	▎light	▎heat
▎가장 가까운	▎중심	▎태양계	▎행성
▎궤도를 돌다	▎~을 회전하다	▎몇 배	▎크기가 더 큰

 **Question** **Vocabulary I**

Let's make sentences by filling in the blanks, using the words below.

Words

PLANET(▶) / SUN(▼) / CLOSE(▲) / WEIGH(◀)

EARTH(▲) / ROTATE (◀)

Let's find the matching words.

| Interesting | Fact | Light | Orbit | Mostly |

(a) 빛   (   )

(b) 궤도를 돌다   (   )

(c) 재미있는   (   )

(d) 주로   (   )

(e) 사실   (   )

04 Question **Comprehension**

Look at the sentences below. Decide if they are true or false!

(a) Without the sun, there would be no life on Earth.   O / X

(b) The sun is the farthest star to the Earth.   O / X

(c) The Earth rotates around the sun every 365 days.   O / X

(d) The sun is about 100 times smaller than the Earth.   O / X

Recycling Is Important!

The Earth is our home. Many people live on Earth. It is a beautiful place. But sadly, it is sick now. Many animals and plants are dying. The air and water are becoming dirty. We have to do something before it's too late!

So, what can we do to save the Earth? There are many things we can do. Recycling is one of the most important things. Recycling is easy! Do not throw away glass bottles, cans, and newspapers. They can be used again. Ask your mom or dad about recycling. They can help you save the Earth! Today, think about the ways to recycle with your family!

Staff reporter Erica Choi

Complete the sentences by filling in the blanks.

(a) Earth is a **b** __ __ __ __ __ __ __ place but it is **s** __ __ __ now.

(b) Many animals and **p** __ __ __ __ __ are dying and the air and water are becoming **d** __ __ __ __.

(c) By **r** __ __ __ __ __ __ __ __ I can **s** __ __ __ the Earth.

(d) I will **t** __ __ __ __ about **w** __ __ __ to recycle with my family.

Word Tip			
▌Earth	▌sadly	▌plant	▌have to
_____	_____	_____	_____
▌save	▌재활용	▌~중 하나	▌버리다
_____	_____	_____	_____
▌유리병	▌깡통	▌사용되다	
_____	_____	_____	

 **Vocabulary I**

Let's complete the crossword puzzle.

Words

RECYCLING (▼) / BEAUTIFUL (▶) / THROW (▼)
ANIMAL (▶) / BOTTLE (▶) / HELP (▼)

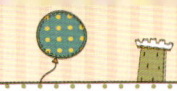

 **Question 03** **Vocabulary Ⅱ**

Let's find the matching words.

| Recycling | Throw away | Save | Important | Sick |

(a) 구하다 ( )

(b) 중요한 ( )

(c) 재활용 ( )

(d) 아픈 ( )

(e) 버리다 ( )

 **Question 04** **Comprehension**

Look at the sentences below. Circle **O** if the statement is true, and circle **X** if the statement is false.

(a) Many people live on Earth.   **O / X**

(b) Recycling is not very important.   **O / X**

(c) The air and water are becoming clean.   **O / X**

(d) We should think about the ways to recycle with our families.   **O / X**

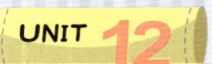

Good Table Manners Are Important

We eat three times a day. Sometimes we eat out at restaurants. When we eat with other people, it is important to maintain good table manners.

Say "Thank you." when your food is served. Do not start eating until food is served to everyone. Eat with your fork and spoon or chopsticks. Don't use your fingers. Also, eat your food with your mouth closed. Do not make loud noises while chewing. And do not speak when your mouth is full of food. Eat your food slowly, while enjoying the taste. If the food is too big, cut it into smaller pieces. Do not complain about the food even if you don't like it. When you need to go to the restroom, say "Excuse me." Always keep good table manners!

Staff reporter Erica Choi

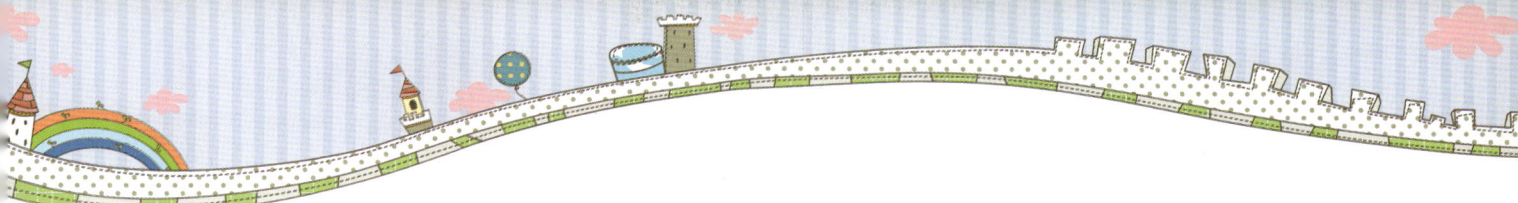

Complete the sentences by filling in the blanks.

(a) Hi, my name is Amy. Today I am _____ a hamburger with some French fries for lunch.

(b) My mother always tells me that it is important to _____ good table manners.

(c) You should always say "_____" when your food is served.

(d) Sometimes you might not like the food. But you shouldn't _____ about it.

(e) Always try to chew your food slowly and enjoy the _____.

Word Tip			
▪ sometimes	▪ eat out	▪ maintain	▪ be served
_____	_____	_____	_____
▪ chopsticks	▪ finger	▪ loud noise	▪ 씹다
_____	_____	_____	_____
▪ ~으로 가득 차다	▪ 맛	▪ 조각	▪ 불평하다
_____	_____	_____	_____
▪ 화장실			
_____			

 **Question** **Vocabulary I**

Let's learn how to spell the important words in the article!

(a) **C** __ __ __ __ __ __ __ __

(b) **L** __ __ __

(c) **P** __ __ __ __

(d) **A** __ __ __ __ __

 **Question** **Vocabulary II**

Find the right words below and fill in the blanks.

Burger / Car / Ice cream / Spoon / Chair / Hot dog
Pizza / Pencil / Umbrella / Exercise / Phone

(a) **B** __ __ __ __ __

(b) **I** __ __ __ __ __ __ __

(c) **S** __ __ __ __

(d) **H** __ __ __ __ __

(e) **P** __ __ __ __

Let's Learn about Chocolate!

Do you like eating chocolate? Many people all over the world love chocolate. But how much do you know about it?

Did you know that chocolate has a long history? The Maya Indians started eating it in 600 AD. They thought it was good for their health. Cocoa beans were very valuable a long time ago. They were once used as money. They were also given as gifts for special days.

Chocolate can give you energy. Dark chocolate is better than milk chocolate. Milk chocolate has more fat and sugar than dark chocolate. Many doctors say eating dark chocolate can make your heart stronger.

Staff reporter Daniel Chang

 **01** Question **Comprehension**

Let's look at the picture and fill in the blanks.

Hint: Answers are in the article.

(a) Many **p** __ __ __ __ __ like **e** __ __ __ __ __ __ chocolate.

(b) Cocoa beans were very **v** __ __ __ __ __ __ __ a long time ago.

(c) Cocoa beans once **u** __ __ __ as **m** __ __ __ __.

(d) Dark chocolate is **b** __ __ __ __ __ than milk chocolate.

(e) Eating dark **c** __ __ __ __ __ __ __ __ can make your heart

　　s __ __ __ __ __ __ __ .

Word Tip			
▌like ~ing	▌all over the world	▌history	▌good for
_____	_____	_____	_____
▌건강	▌귀중한, 가치 있는	▌오래 전에	
_____	_____	_____	

 **Vocabulary**

Connect each picture to the correct meaning.

history

ⓐ

① powerful, opposite of weak

valuable

ⓑ

② a record of events or people

strong

ⓒ

③ precious, important

 **Question** **Writing**

Look at the picture below and write your answers.

Hint: Be creative!

(a) What do you think is in the box?

→ I think there is **c** __ __ __ __ __ __ __ __ in the **b** __ __.

(b) Why is the box on the bench?

→ Someone **l** __ __ __ the box on the **b** __ __ __ __ by accident.

(c) Who would you give it to?

→ I would like to **g** __ __ __ the chocolate to my **m** __ __.

Let's Shake Hands!

We often shake hands with other people. But do you know why people shake hands? When did people start shaking hands? Today, let's learn about the history of the handshake.

People started shaking hands a long time ago. In the Middle Ages, knights showed and held each others' hands to show that they didn't have any weapons. They shook hands to mean no harm to each other. Today, handshaking is used to greet or congratulate another person. When you shake hands with other people, always use your right hand. Using the left hand is rude. Hold the other person's hand firmly while looking at their eyes.

Staff reporter Dan Chun

 **Question** **Vocabulary**

Read the questions and answer the following.

(a) Look at the words below.

> Vitamin   Knights   Weapon   Create   Harm   Safety

Which words can be used to talk about the history of handshakes? Choose three words.

_____, _____, _____

(b) Find the three words that start with "S" in the article.

① _____

② _____

③ _____

(c) Which word has the opposite meaning to "Harm"?

G __ __ __

Word Tip			
▌often	▌shake hands with	▌handshake	▌knight
_____	_____	_____	_____
▌show	▌held	▌무기	▌해, 손상
_____	_____	_____	_____
▌인사하다	▌축하하다	▌무례한	▌단단히, 굳게
_____	_____	_____	_____
▌~을 보다			
_____			

 **Question** **Writing**

Let's make sentences by filling in the blanks, using the words below.

congratulate / using / greet / learn / often / history

(a) We __ __ __ __ __ shake hands with other people __ __ __ __ __ the right hand.

(b) This week, let's __ __ __ __ __ about the __ __ __ __ __ __ __ of the handshake.

(c) Today, handshaking is used to __ __ __ __ __ or __ __ __ __ __ __- __ __ __ __ __ __ __ another person.

03 **Question** **Comprehension**

Look at the pictures. Mark "O" for the pictures that look polite. Mark "X" for the pictures that look impolite.

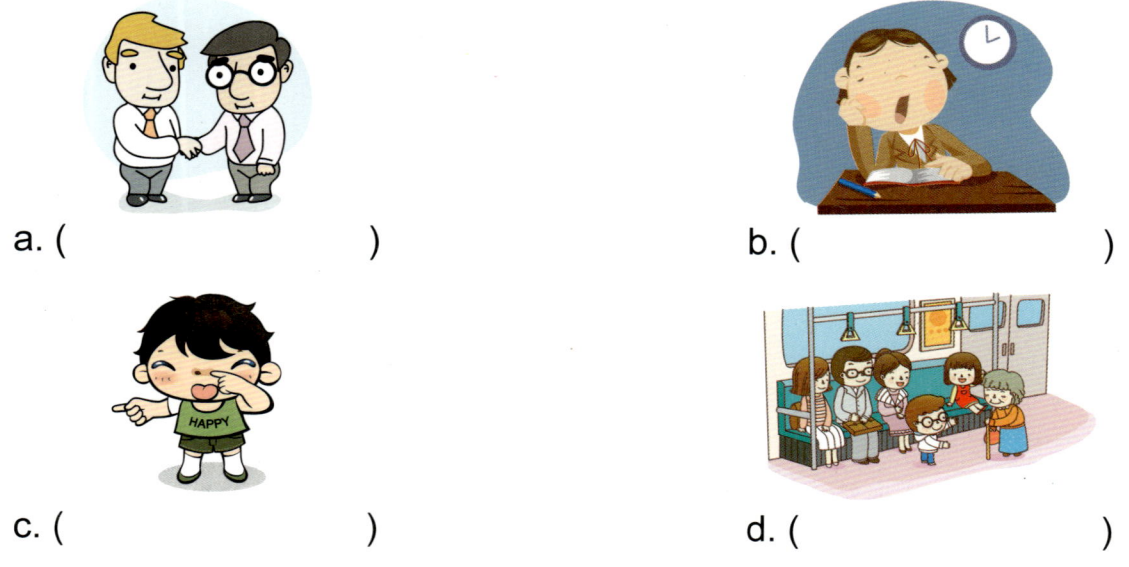

a. (   )

b. (   )

c. (   )

d. (   )

04 Question Structure

Match up the pictures and words to make the right sentences.

Today, handshaking is used ⓐ

① to greet or congratulate another person.

When you shake hands with ⓑ other people

② while looking at their eyes.

People started shaking hands ⓒ

③ always use your right hand.

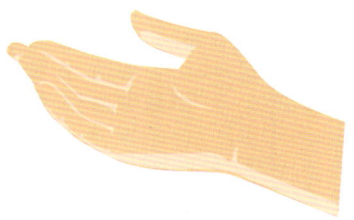

Hold the other person's hand firmly ⓓ

④ a long time ago.

The History of Soap

We use soap every day. We wash our hands with it. Soap keeps our hands clean. So we have to say "Thank you." to soap! Today, let's learn about the history of soap.

People started using soap about 2,000 years ago in Pompeii, Italy. Soap was made by boiling animal fat or vegetable oils with wood ashes. At the time, soap was very expensive. Only the rich could use it. In 1790, a French chemist named Nicholas Leblanc found a new way to make soap easily and quickly. Thanks to him, many people in Europe could buy inexpensive soap.

Staff reporter Samuel Sohn

Let's look at the picture. Fill in the blanks and complete the sentences.

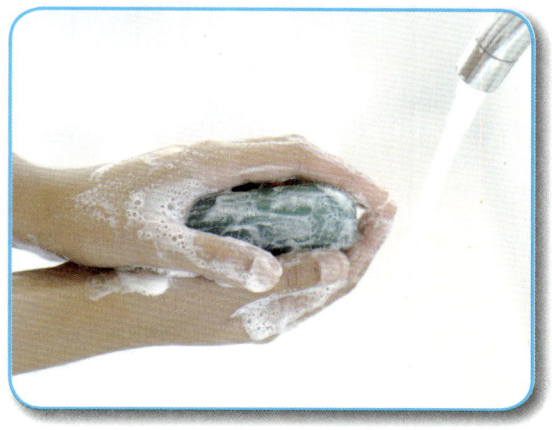

clean
soap
say
history
wash

(a) We use (　　　　) every day.

(b) We (　　　　) our hands with soap.

(c) Soap keeps our hands (　　　　).

(d) We have to (　　　　) "Thank you." to soap.

(e) Let's learn about the (　　　　) of soap.

Word Tip

▌wash one's hands	▌keep	▌have to	▌learn
_____	_____	_____	_____
▌history	▌Pompeii	▌boil	▌animal fat
_____	_____	_____	_____
▌vegetable oil	▌wood ash	▌그 당시에는	▌비싼
_____	_____	_____	_____
▌부자들	▌프랑스인	▌화학자	▌~라는 이름의, ~라 불리는
_____	_____	_____	_____
▌발견하다	▌방법	▌쉽게	▌빠르게
_____	_____	_____	_____
▌~덕분에	▌저렴한, 비싸지 않은		
_____	_____		

 **Grammar**

Circle the right word to make the sentence correct.

(a) People started [**using** / **to use** / **used**] soap about 2,000 years ago in Pompeii, Italy.

(b) Soap was made [**at** / **by** / **from**] boiling animal fat or vegetable oils with wood ashes.

(c) At the time, soap was [**more** / **very** / **much**] expensive.

(d) In 1790, a French chemist found a new way to make soap [**easily** / **easy** / **ease**] and quickly.

(e) Thanks to the chemist, many people in Europe could [**bought** / **buying** / **buy**] inexpensive soap.

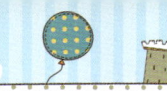

 **Vocabulary**

Find the hidden words in the puzzle below. The words are from the article.

M	A	G	L	W	S	W	D	R	O
G	D	O	Q	A	V	I	B	V	I
N	J	G	B	S	G	G	O	C	E
L	I	G	C	H	E	M	I	S	T
H	T	G	N	U	E	L	T	M	
J	V	Y	R	E	F	R	F	A	N
S	T	Y	K	T	H	G	I	R	B
P	O	A	C	R	L	W	Q	H	E
P	B	A	O	W	Y	Q	S	G	F
Q	E	X	P	E	N	S	I	V	E

Words

SOAP / WASH / BOIL
EXPENSIVE / CHEMIST

ANSWERS

Word Tip

가장 나이 많은 / 쌍둥이 / 태어나다 / ~하는 것을 즐기다 / 비밀 / live a long life / laughter / laugh / like

1. Writing I
   (a) the oldest twins
   (b) 101 years
   (c) laughter

2. Grammar
   (a) on
   (b) healthy
   (c) shopping
   (d) like

3. Writing II
What do you think about the grandmothers in the picture? Don't they look alike? Don't be surprised; They are twins! Actually they are the oldest twins in the world! Take a guess how old they are. They became 101 years old in 2011! They spend a lot of time together. They go shopping together every week. They must be rich! Do you know what their secret is? The key to their long life is laughter! So if you want to live healthy and long, laugh a lot!

4. Vocabulary

Word Tip

일하다 / 한국계 미국인 / 미식 축구 선수 / 태어나다 / African - American / choose A as B / advisor / advice

1. Comprehension I
   (a) ①
   (b) For / Football / Father
   (c) advices

2. Vocabulary
   (a) ③
   (b) ④
   (c) ④

3. Comprehension II
   (a) ①
   (b) ③
   (c) ③

Word Tip

맛있는 / 패스트푸드 / 음식점 / 팔다 / waffle / gain huge popularity / among / soon

1. Vocabulary I
   (a) around
   (b) enjoy
   (c) opened
   (d) popularity
   (e) soon

2. Vocabulary II
   ⓐ – ②
   ⓑ – ①
   ⓒ – ③

3. Writing
   (a) at a fast food restaurant
   (b) hamburgers, fish burgers, and waffles
   (c) gaining huge popularity

Word Tip

여행하다 / 장소 / 어딘가에 / 재미 / 멋진, 훌륭한 / 휴식을 취하다 / 기회 / have fun / of course / something new / plan / train / airplane

1. Conversation
   (a) travel, fun
   (b) relax, chance
   (c) somewhere, something
   (d) learn, meet
   (e) even, family

2. Vocabulary I
   (a) Travel
   (b) Rest
   (c) Chance
   (d) Plan

3. Vocabulary II
   (a) Tent
   (b) Airplane
   (c) Barbeque
   (d) Relax
   (e) Camera

Word Tip

생일 / 축하하다, 기념하다 / 전 세계에 / 초대하다 / delicious / receive / Why don't you ~? / plan

1. Vocabulary
   (a) Cake, Gift, Card
   (b) Friend / Family / Food
   (c) Give

2. Writing
   (a) celebrate
   (b) delicious, friends
   (c) invite, special

3. Comprehension
   (a) O

(b) X
(c) O
(d) X

4. Structure
ⓐ – ③, ⓑ – ④
ⓒ – ①, ⓓ – ②

UNIT **06**

Word Tip

애완동물 / 실제로 / 건강 / ~에 따르면 /
(시간을) 보내다 / 방법 / 소유자 /
feel better / find / study /
calm down / be stressed / soon /
feel down

1. Vocabulary
(a) Pet
(b) Peanut / Peace / Pick
(c) Spending time with a pet
    makes people happy.

2. Writing
(a) health
(b) spending, beat
(c) down, walk

3. Comprehension
(a) O
(b) X
(c) X
(d) O

4. Structure
ⓐ – ②
ⓑ – ③
ⓒ – ①

UNIT **07**

Word Tip

가을 / 계절 / 자전거 / 타다 / ~에 좋다 /
건강 / 기다리다 / ~해야 한다 / safely /
wear / helmet / protect / bright /
clothes / road / easily

---

1. Writing
(a) protect
(b) health
(c) bright

2. Comprehension
(a) X
(b) X
(c) O

3. Vocabulary I
(a) head
(b) health
(c) safe

4. Vocabulary II

A	B	R	T	E	S	G	E	R	S
P	D	G	H	I	G	H	F	J	D
O	B	T	S	E	A	S	O	N	N
W	Q	H	J	K	M	A	O	U	V
T	E	R	T	G	H	F	I	U	B
U	P	P	R	O	T	E	C	T	O
L	O	U	I	F	H	N	D	H	H
A	V	D	F	E	G	J	K	L	U
N	C	V	B	R	I	G	H	T	L
E	B	N	M	H	D	S	A	W	E

UNIT **08**

Word Tip

9월 / 여전히 / 낮 동안에 / 아침에 /
밤에 / 가을 / 계절 / 완벽한 / 중요한 /
learn / world history / famous /
culture / wonderful / choose

1. Vocabulary
(a) Books
(b) Body / Baby / Back / Beach
(c) Children can learn many
    things from books.

2. Writing
(a) perfect
(b) history, cultures
(c) choose

---

3. Comprehension
(a) O
(b) X

4. Structure
ⓐ – ①
ⓑ – ③
ⓒ – ②

UNIT **09**

Word Tip

곤경에 처하다 / 실수하다 / 사실 /
완벽한 / admit / be careful / way /
solve problems

1. Vocabulary
(a) Admit, Careful, Learn
(b) Make / Many / Mistake
(c) Different

2. Writing
(a) fact, learn
(b) mistake, same
(c) admit

3. Comprehension
(a) O
(b) O
(c) X
(d) X

4. Structure
ⓐ – ①, ⓑ – ④
ⓒ – ③, ⓓ – ②

UNIT **10**

Word Tip

~을 보다 / 매일 / 흥미로운 / 사실 /
~없이 / 생명체 / 빛 / 열 / the closest /
center / Solar System / planet /
orbit / rotate / times / bigger than

1. Writing
(a) much
(b) most

(c) heat
(d) center
(e) made

2. Vocabulary I

3. Vocabulary II
(a) Light
(b) Orbit
(c) Interesting
(d) Mostly
(e) Fact

4. Comprehension
(a) O
(b) X
(c) O
(d) X

UNIT 11

Word Tip
지구 / 슬프게 / 식물 / 해야 한다 /
구하다 / recycling / one of ~ /
throw away / glass bottle / can /
be used

1. Writing
(a) beautiful, sick
(b) plants, dirty
(c) recycling, save
(d) think, ways

2. Vocabulary I

3. Vocabulary II
(a) Save
(b) Important
(c) Recycling
(d) Sick
(e) Throw away

4. Comprehension
(a) O
(b) X
(c) X
(d) O

UNIT 12

Word Tip
때때로 / 외식하다 / 유지하다 / 나오다 /
젓가락 / 손가락 / 시끄러운 소음 /
chew / be full of ~ / taste / piece /
complain / restroom

1. Conversation
(a) eating
(b) have (maintain)
(c) Thank you
(d) complain
(e) taste

2. Vocabulary I
(a) Chopsticks
(b) Loud
(c) Piece
(d) Always

3. Vocabulary II
(a) Burger
(b) Ice cream
(c) Spoon
(d) Hot dog
(e) Pizza

UNIT 13

Word Tip
~하는 것을 좋아하다 / 전 세계에 /
역사 / ~에 좋은 / health / valuable /
a long time ago

1. Comprehension
(a) people, eating
(b) valuable
(c) used, money
(d) better
(e) chocolate, stronger

2. Vocabulary
ⓐ – ②
ⓑ – ③
ⓒ – ①

3. Writing
(a) chocolate, box
(b) left, bench
(c) give, mom

UNIT 14

Word Tip
종종, 자주 / 악수하다 / 악수 / 기사 /
보여주다 / 잡았다 / weapon / harm /
greet / congratulate / rude /
firmly / look at

1. Vocabulary
(a) Knights, Weapon, Harm
(b) Shake / Start / Show
(c) Good

2. Writing
(a) often, using

(b) learn, history
(c) greet, congratulate

3. Comprehension

(a) O
(b) X
(c) X
(d) O

4. Structure

ⓐ – ①, ⓑ – ③
ⓒ – ④, ⓓ – ②

3. Vocabulary

M	A	G	L	W	S	W	D	R	O
G	D	O	Q	A	V	I	B	V	I
N	J	G	B	S	G	G	O	C	E
L	I	G	C	H	E	M	I	S	T
H	T	G	N	U	E	L	T	M	
J	V	Y	R	E	F	R	F	A	N
S	T	Y	K	T	H	G	I	R	B
P	O	A	C	R	L	W	Q	H	E
P	B	A	O	W	Y	Q	S	G	F
Q	E	X	P	E	N	S	I	V	E

UNIT **15**

Word Tip

~의 손을 씻다 / 유지하다 / 해야 한다 /
배우다 / 역사 / 폼페이 / 끓이다 /
동물성 지방 / 식물성 지방 / 나뭇재 /
at the time / expensive /
the rich / French / chemist /
named / find / way / easily /
quickly / thanks to / inexpensive

1. Writing

(a) soap
(b) wash
(c) clean
(d) say
(e) history

2. Grammar

(a) using
(b) by
(c) very
(d) easily
(e) buy